T0080984

Bedřich Smetana

(1824–1884)

Die Moldau

Für Klavier leicht bearbeitet von
Hans-Günter Heumann

Zeichnungen von Brigitte Smith

The Moldau

In a simple arrangement for piano by
Hans-Günter Heumann

English translation by Julia Rushworth
Drawings by Brigitte Smith

ED 23595
ISMN 979-0-001-21610-4
ISBN 978-3-7957-2684-3

Mainz · London · Madrid · Paris · New York · Tokyo · Beijing
© 1998/2022 Schott Music GmbH & Co. KG, Mainz · Printed in Germany
www.schott-music.com

Liebe Klavierspielerin,
lieber Klavierspieler,

in diesem Band wird das instrumentale Meisterwerk *Die Moldau* des tschechischen Komponisten Bedřich (Friedrich) Smetana (1824–1884) in leichter Bearbeitung für Klavier vorgestellt.

Von 1874–1879 komponierte Smetana (er war bereits vollständig taub) den Zyklus sinfonischer Dichtungen für Orchester *Mein Vaterland*, eine Hymne auf seine Heimat Böhmen. Der populärste Part des Zyklus ist der zweite Teil *Die Moldau*, in der der Komponist den Weg des Flusses von der Quelle bis zu seiner Einmündung in die Elbe nachzeichnet.

Smetana schreibt über sein Werk:
„Diese Komposition schildert den Lauf der Moldau. Sie belauscht ihre zwei Quellen, die ,warme' und die ,kalte' Moldau, verfolgt dann ihre Vereinigung und den Lauf des Stromes durch Wiesen und Haine, durch Gegenden, wo die Bewohner gerade fröhlich Feste feiern. Im silbernen Mondlicht führen Wassernymphen ihre Reigen auf, stolze Burgen, Schlösser und ehrwürdige Ruinen, mit den wilden Felsen verwachsen, ziehen vorbei. Die Moldau schäumt und wirbelt in den Stromschnellen zu St. Johann, strömt in breitem Fluß weiter auf Prag zu, die Burg Vyšehrad taucht auf an ihrem Ufer. Die Moldau strebt majestätisch weiter, entschwindet den Blicken und ergießt sich schließlich in die Elbe."

Aber nun tretet ein in die zauberhafte Heimat Smetanas und macht eine abenteuerliche musikalische Fahrt auf dem Hauptfluss Böhmens.

Euer
Hans-Günter Heumann

Dear Pianists,

In this volume you will find a simple arrangement for piano of the orchestral masterpiece *The Moldau* by the Czech composer Bedřich (Frederick) Smetana (1824–1884).

Between 1874 and 1879 Smetana (who was already completely deaf) composed the cycle of symphonic poems for orchestra *My Fatherland*, a hymn of praise to his homeland of Bohemia. The most popular part of the cycle is the second part, *The Moldau*, in which the composer traces the path of the river from its source to where it flows out into the Elbe.

Smetana wrote of his work:
'This composition follows the course of the Moldau. We hear the sounds of its two sources of origin, the 'warm' and the 'cold' water streams which are then united and flow through meadows and groves, and on through places where country folk are celebrating their festivals. Water nymphs perform their dances in the silvery moonlight; we float past proud fortresses, fine castles and noble ruins, overgrown like the craggy rocks on which they stand. The Moldau froths and eddies over the rapids of St Johann, then streams on in a broad torrent towards Prague, with the castle of Vyšehrad coming into sight on its bank. The Moldau surges majestically onward, disappearing from view and finally flowing into the Elbe.'

And now step inside the magical world of Smetana's homeland and take a musical adventure trip along Bohemia's most important river.

With best wishes,
Hans-Günter Heumann

Inhalt

Contents

Steckbrief
Die Moldau

Gesamtwerk „Mein Vaterland", Zyklus einer sechsteiligen sinfonischen Dichtung (Nr. 2 „Die Moldau")

komponiert 20. November bis 8. Dezember 1874 in Prag

uraufgeführt 4. April 1875 in Prag

Orchesterbesetzung Piccoloflöte, 2 Flöten, 2 Oboen, 2 Klarinetten, 2 Fagotte, 4 Hörner, 2 Trompeten, 3 Posaunen, Bass-tuba, Pauken, Schlagzeug (Triangel, Becken, große Trommel), Harfe, Streicher

History of the Work
The Moldau

Taken fom 'My Fatherland', a sequence of pieces in the form of a six-part symphonic poem (No. 2 is entitled 'The Moldau')

Composed in Prague between 20 November and 8 December 1874

First performed in Prague on 4 April 1875

Orchestral scoring piccolo, 2 flutes, 2 oboes, 2 clarinets, 2 bassoons, 4 horns, 2 trumpets, 3 trombones, bass tuba, timpani, percussion (triangle, cymbals, bass drum), harp, strings

Steckbrief
Bedřich (Friedrich) Smetana

1824 geboren am 2. März in Leitomischl (Böhmen)

1830 erstes öffentliches Konzert

seit 1843 studierte er Klavier und Musiktheorie an der Musikschule von Joseph Proksch und wurde Konzertpianist.

1848 Gründung einer eigenen Musikschule in Prag, die er bis 1856 leitete

1849 Heirat mit Kateřina Kolářová

1856 ging er als Dirigent der Abonnementskonzerte der „Harmoniska Sällskapet" ins schwedische Göteborg. Erste große Werke in Form der sinfonischen Dichtung nach Liszts Muster

1859 Tod seiner Frau

1860 Heirat mit Bettina Ferdinandová

1861 kehrte er in seine Heimat zurück und ließ sich endgültig in Prag als Musikkritiker, Dirigent am Nationaltheater und Chormeister des Männergesangvereins nieder. Hauptsächlich aber widmete er sich der Komposition (Opern, Kammermusik und Orchesterwerke)

1874 wurde er taub und musste vom öffentlichen Musikleben zurücktreten, komponierte aber emsig weiter

1882 es zeigten sich erste Anzeichen geistiger Umnachtung

1884 Einweisung in eine Prager Irrenanstalt, dort starb er am 12. Mai

Biography
Bedřich (Frederick) Smetana

1824 born in Leitomischl (Bohemia) on 2 March

1830 gave his first public concert performance

1843 onwards studied the piano and music theory at the Joseph Proksch Academy of Music, becoming a concert pianist

1848 founded his own music school in Prague, remaining there as principal until 1856

1849 married Kateřina Kolářová

1856 went to Göteborg in Sweden as conductor of the concert series of the 'Harmoniska Sällskapet'. Composed his first large-scale works in the form of symphonic poems, in the tradition of Liszt

1859 death of his wife

1860 married Bettina Ferdinandová

1861 returned to his homeland and settled in Prague as music critic, conductor at the National Theatre and chorus master of the Prague male voice choir. Devoted most of his energies to composition, however (operas, chember music and orchestral works)

1874 became deaf and had to retire from performing as a musician, but went on composing prolifically

1882 appearance of first signs of mental derangement

1884 committed to lunatic asylum in Prague, where he died on 12 May

Die Quelle der Moldau
The Source of the Moldau

Allegro commodo non agitato ♩. = 60

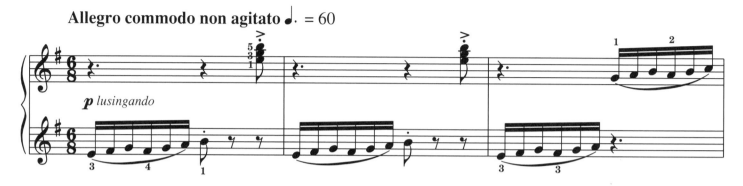

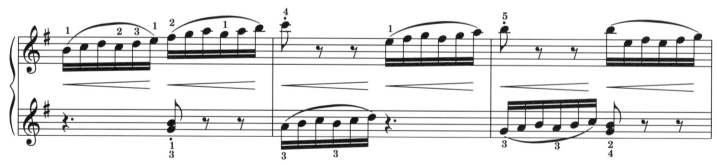

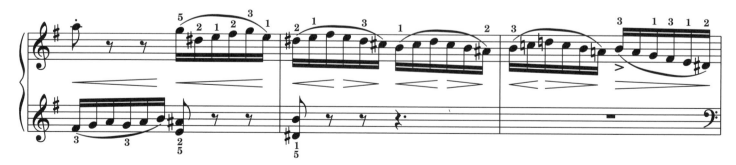

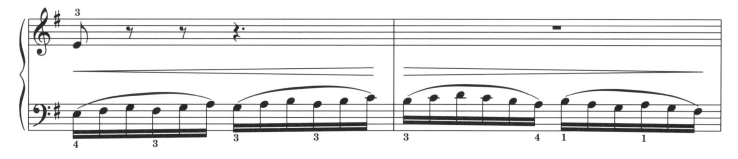

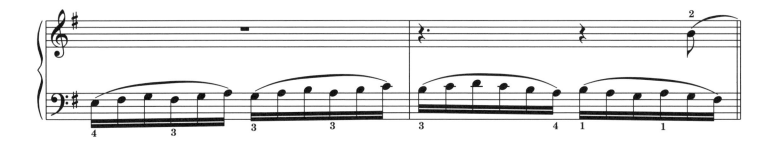

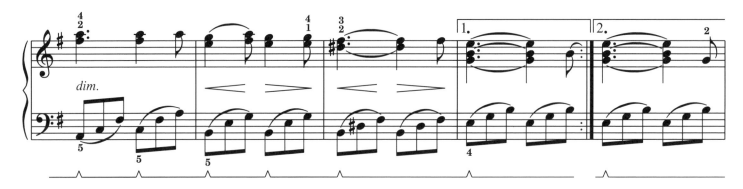

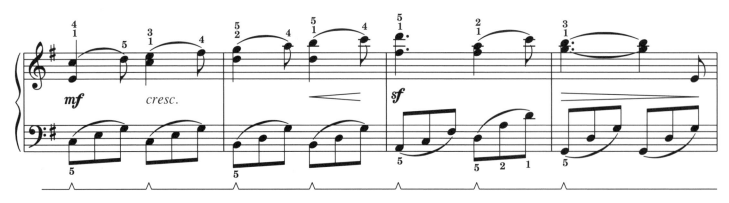

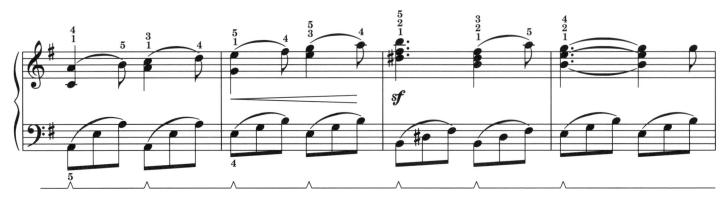

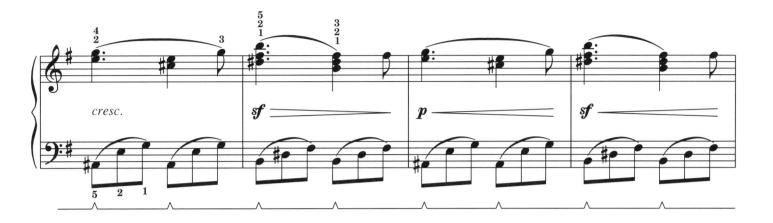

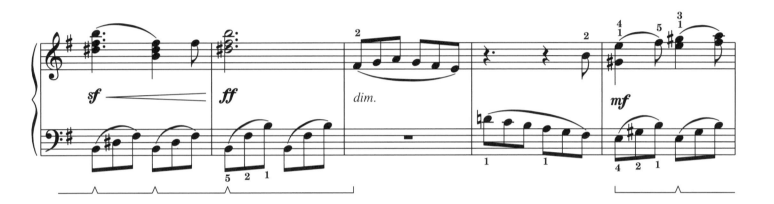

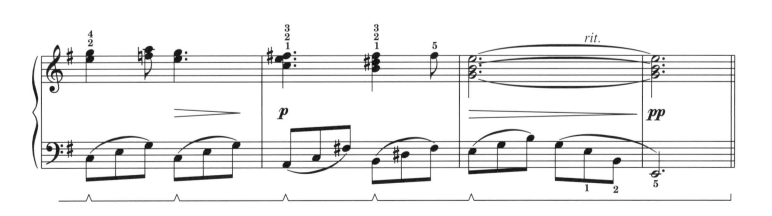

Waldjagd
Hunting in the Forest

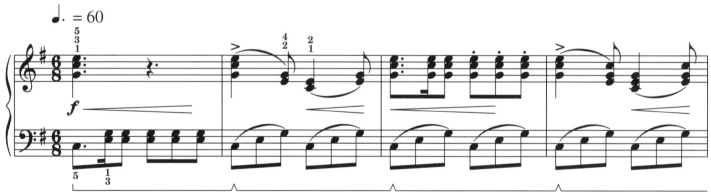

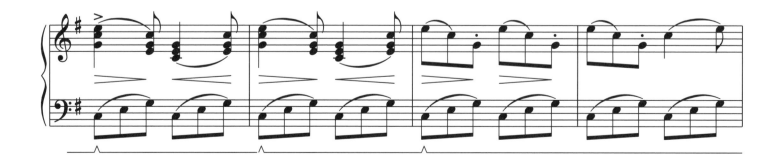

Hochzeit auf dem Lande
A Country Wedding

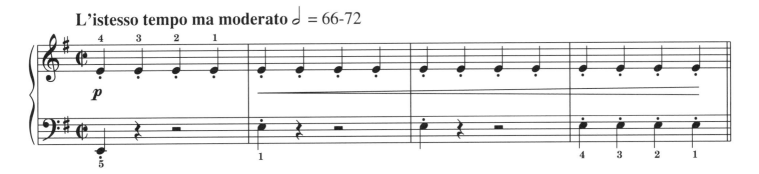

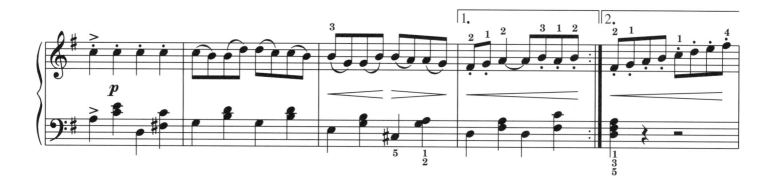

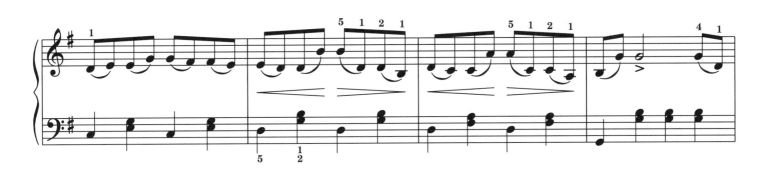

Elfentanz im Mondschein
Elves Dance in the Moonlight

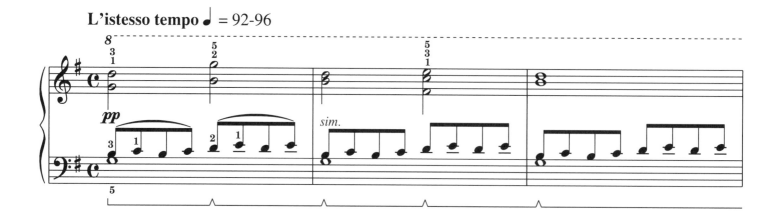

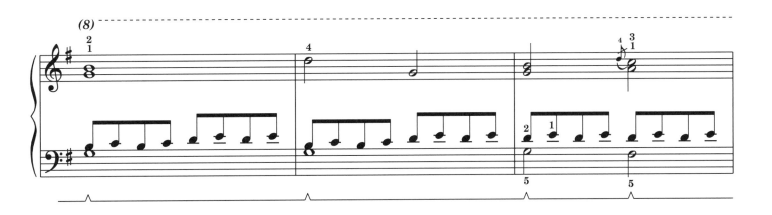

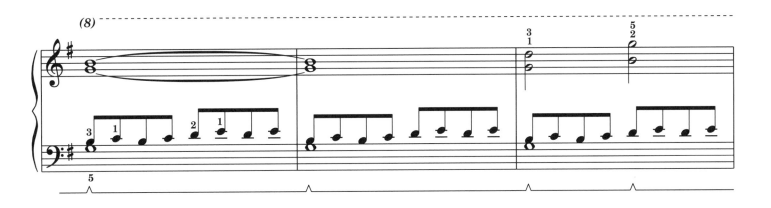

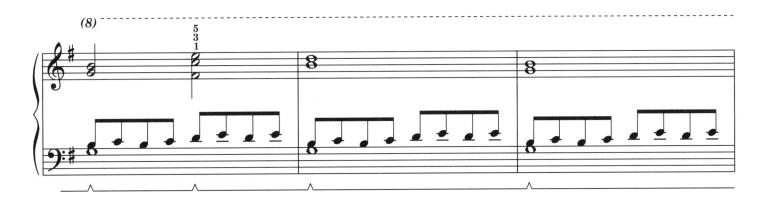

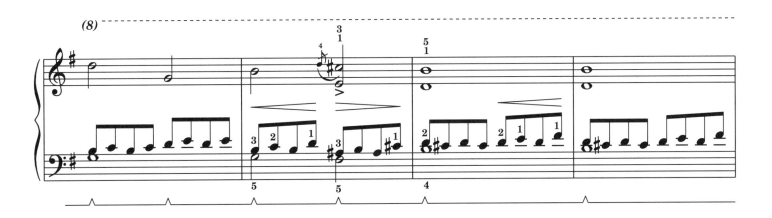

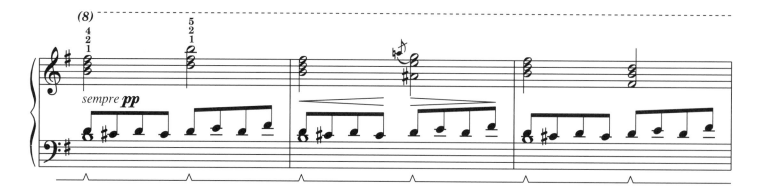

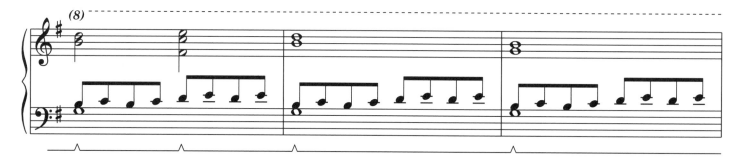

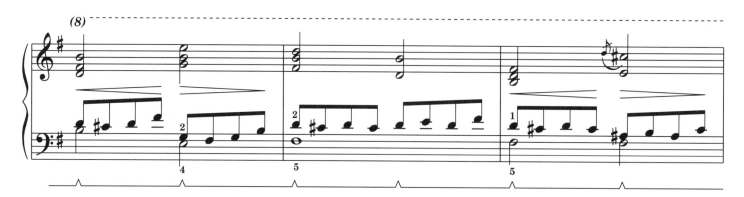

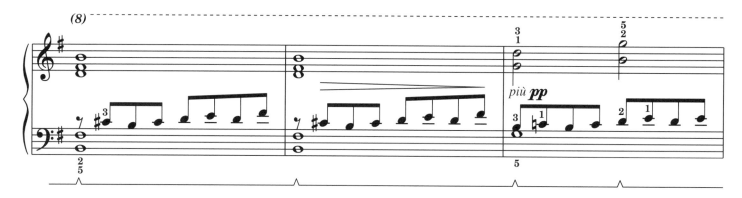

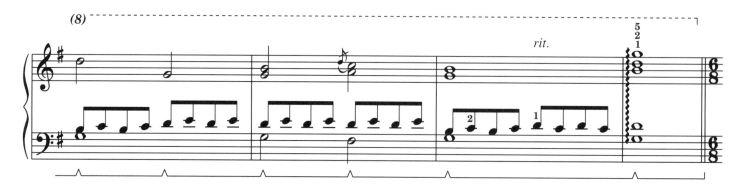

Allegro commodo non agitato ♩. = 60

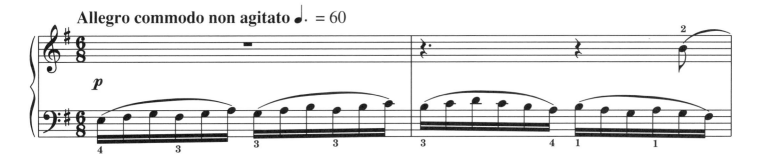

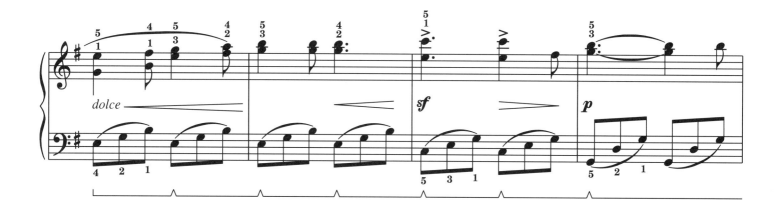

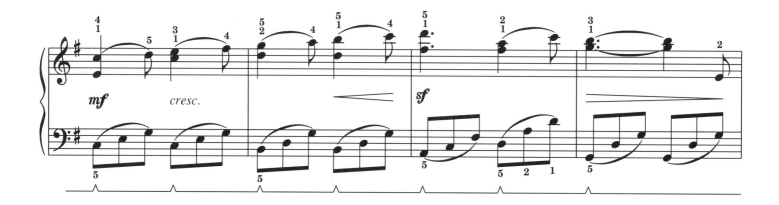

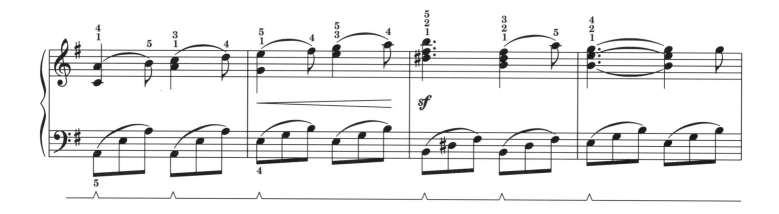

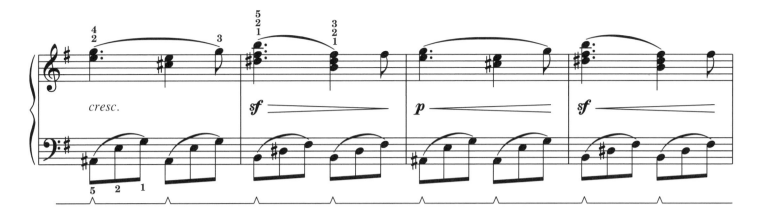

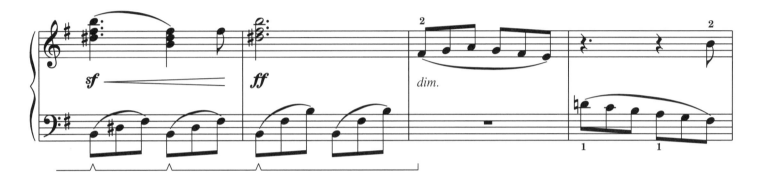

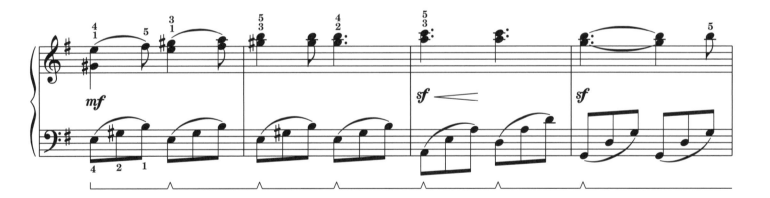

Stromschnellen von St. Johann
The Rapids of St Johann

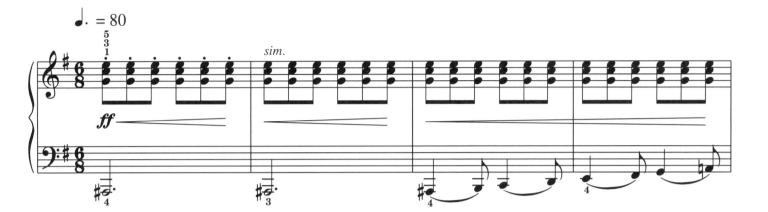

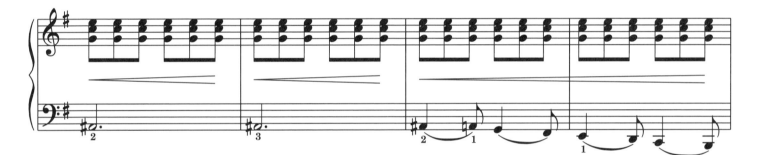

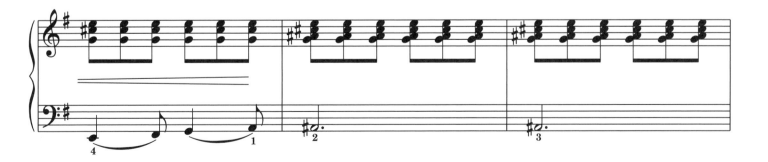

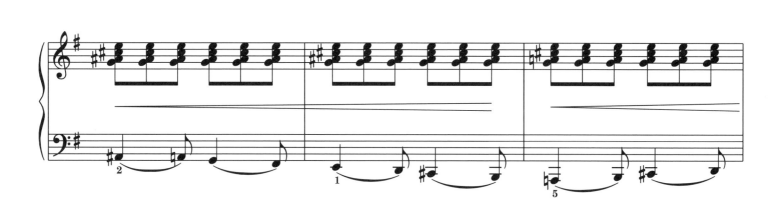

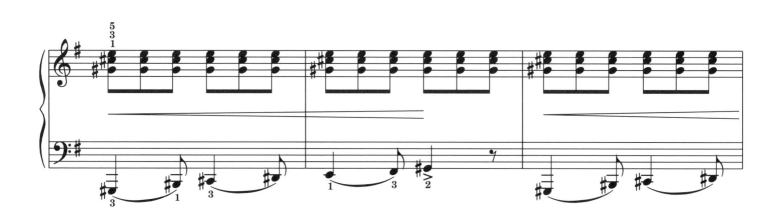

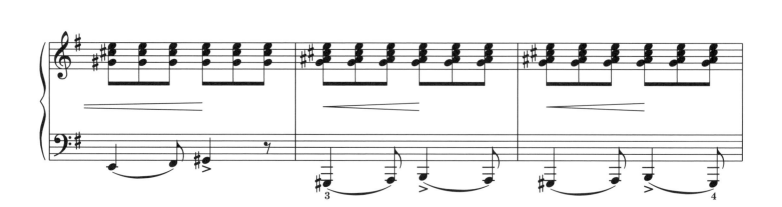

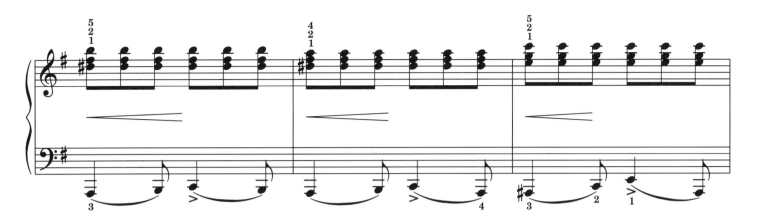

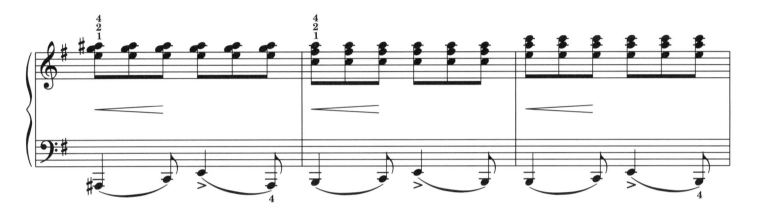

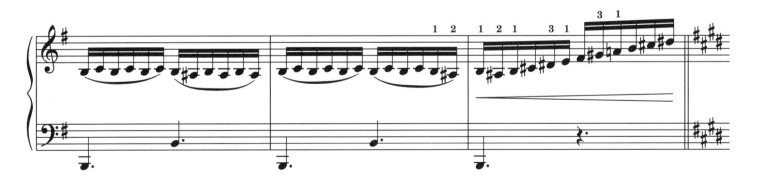

Breit fließt der Strom
The River Flows Wide

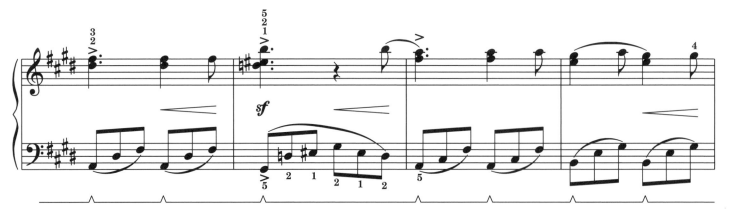

Vyšehrad-Motiv
A Vision of Vyšehrad

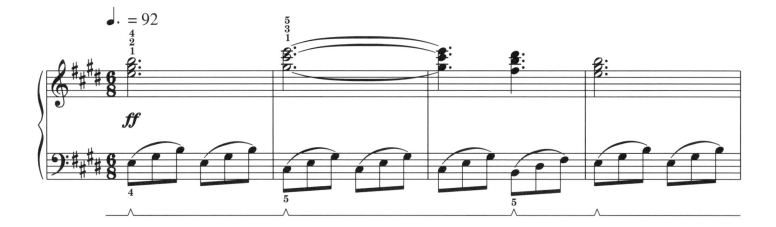

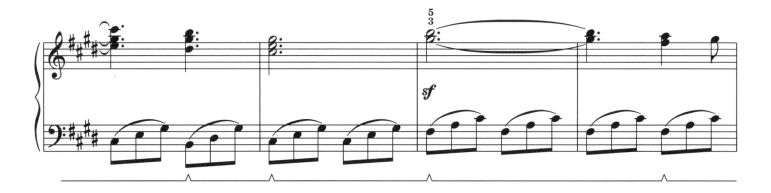

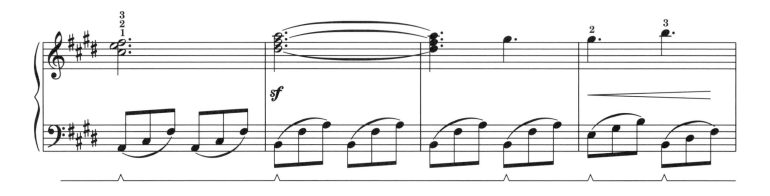

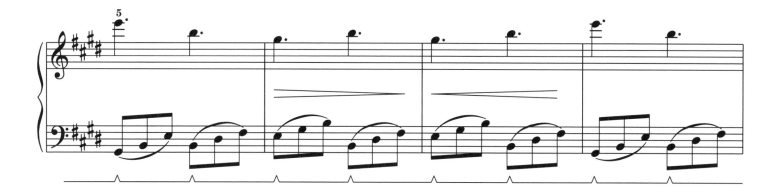

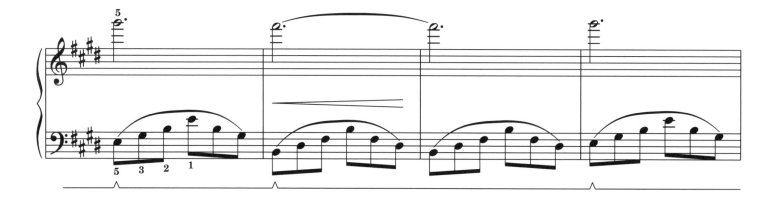

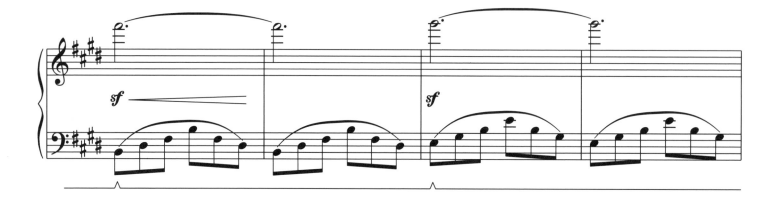

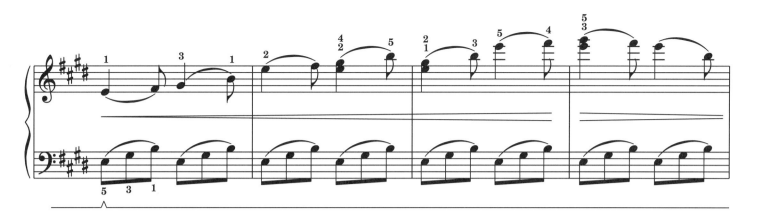

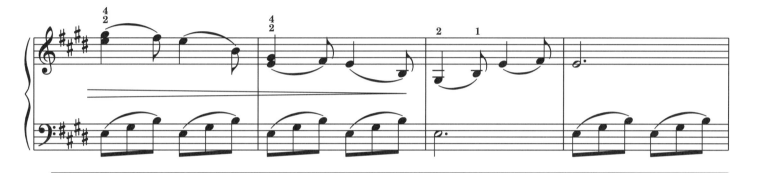

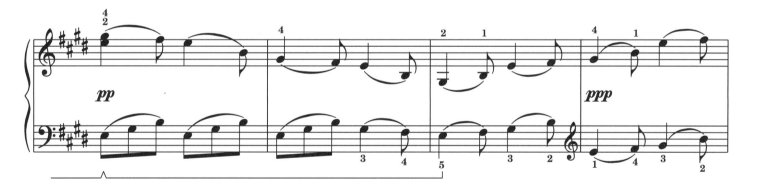

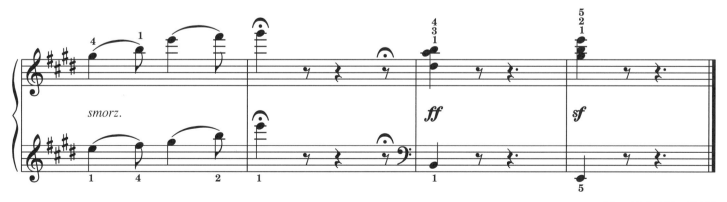

Schott Music, Mainz 60 147